I
Breathe To Love You

Entangled Dreams

Antonio Fleming

Iqra Publishing Inc.

Printed in the United States of America
First Printing 2025
First Edition 2025
ISBN: 978-1-955393-03-4

Published & Distributed by:
Iqra Publishing Inc.
157 Sunset Avenue
Atlanta, GA 30314
www.iqrapublishing.com
Edited by Chief Editor: Lori McCaskill of the IPI team.

IN THE NAME OF
GOD
THE COMPASSIONATE, THE ALL MERCIFUL

All praise and thanks are due to Allah ta'ala alone, the Sustainer and Creator of existence. May the choicest blessings and peace be upon the last of the righteous messengers and prophets,

Muhammad ﷺ his family, Companions and all those who follow in his footsteps till the

blowing of the trumpet.

قُلْ إِنَّمَا أَنَا بَشَرٌ مِثْلُكُمْ يُوحَى إِلَيَّ أَنَّمَا إِلَهُكُمْ إِلهٌ وَاحِدٌ فَمَن كَانَ يَرْجُو لِقَاءَ رَ بِهِ فَ لَيَعْمَلْ عَمَ الَّ صَالِ احا وَلَّ يشَّرِكُ بِعِبَادَةَ رَ بِهِ أَحَداا ﴿١١٠﴾

Say: "I am only a human being like you. It is revealed to me that your God is One God, therefore whoever wishes

to reach Allah (before death) let him do improving deeds

(the soul's cleansing) and let him not associate anyone with Him in the worship of his Lord".

(Surah Al-Kahf: 110)

Dedication

With boundless love and gratitude, I dedicate this book to Allah Ta'ala, the Most Merciful, who has gifted me the ability to pour my soul into words. Every verse, every emotion, and every reflection within these pages is a testament to the inspiration He has placed within me. Without His divine guidance, this expression of my heart would not exist.

This book is also dedicated to a blessing I have yet to behold—someone whose eyes I have never met, whose heartbeat I have never felt, yet whose presence lives within my dreams. The mere thought of her smile has breathed life into these words, shaping emotions I long to share.

The Prophet Muhammad ﷺ said:

"The most complete of believers in faith are those with the best character, and the best of you are those who are best to their women." (Tirmidhi 1162)

May these words serve as a tribute to love in its purest form—the kind that transcends time, distance, and even reality itself.

Table of Contents

'Thinking'

There are times
when missing you
is a longing within itself
For the tears that splash within my soul
seemingly
are evident in my eyes
Unsuppressed by the sadness
that yokes me as we stand apart
Thinking of you
causes my river to crest and overflow
in a flood of joy.

Whether I'm selfishly
holding you close in my dreams
Intensifying your whispers with my tongue
while you feel
My heart skip a beat
with every sensuous and savory lick
of your private stock of exotic nectar
Or flicking your nipples rapidly
with the coolness of my tongue
as they instantly stand at attention
as though a cold wind brushed them briskly
'Au natural', the quintessential aphrodisiac.

Whether I'm romancing your smile
by feeding you chocolate covered peach slices
beneath millions of distant sparkles of the night
Blanketed by soft cotton beside a roasting fire
as waves crash forcefully against the pier
Or merely secluded in a cove

wallowing in the realm of sincerity
As I lay my head in your lap
tasting your every word
While our eyes connect granting access
deep within our souls
and the softness of your fingers dance upon my chest
Thinking of you
always crests my internal river
overflowing in a flood of joy.

Because I am able to prove($$$$$$$$$$$$$$$$$$)
"I love you!

No matter the illusion
I awaken within myself
All that is important
is the genuine fact:
You know without doubt
"I'm thinking of you"
and suspended in love to infinity.

'Not Missed'

Mystical highlights of the night
pulsate my yearning
When I lay at night center stage in an amphitheater
of millions of stars as my audience
A silent operatic classic
brilliantly sung as Pavarotti
A mental concerto
ingeniously played as though Johannes Sebastian Bach
reverberating within the acoustical lining of my heart
Holding you might just be a fantasy
I cherish far greater than myself
Yet how can I not miss
the dream you will always be
when the stars and constellations are looking on verifiably.

If I painted a picture
of my tears upon the wind
visible to all the continents and the seven seas
they would validate your name scripted in my blood
Captured in awe, an untold number of believers
even the sea creatures
would testify that your smile burns inside my soul
as a white rose within the sun.

Would you think of me
even if it were only a flash of a thought?

When I stand with my face
plastered against my window
Gazing afar to attract answers
that only your whispers can bridge a canyon too impassable

How can I not merge with infinite delusions
granting me your hand
to secure to the right of my lips
Your breath
to write upon with my tongue
and your steps to fill
with the core of my existence
How can I not miss
the dream you will always be.

If your eyes opened
to an Egyptian candle burning
on the threads of your pillow
Strawberries marinating in a glass
of 'Domaine De La Romanée-Conti'
and physically covered
in scripted white rose petals
Which details not only how beautiful you are to me
but also Why you are the Ambassador of my dreams
and why I would never rise from laying beneath your feet
Would you think of me
even in a flash of a thought?

It may storm
outside the window of my dreams
Or it may be cold
standing in this hemisphere entirely alone
Yet no matter the length of steps
I take in the dark
Unfortunately
I will never stop missing
The dream you will always be.

'Not Such Strangers'

When I lay by myself
in the awakening of the morning
I wonder is it you who
suspends the stars in separation
I wonder is it you who
controls the estuary of fresh and salt water
where magically, the two dare not mix
I wonder is it you who
gives the wind strength unyielding.

Secretly, I wonder when I lay by myself
is it you who gives taste to every
dream you're captured within
I wonder as I lay
yet I stand upon assurance
genuine knowledge of that which is true
That you breathe reason into the portals of life.

When the sun hides from your smile
'I listen to you'
In the comforting moments you witness not yourself
'I notice you'
We are not such strangers
as circumstances may imply
For beneath the silence of my words
is a hand woven veil
I lay upon your wings in the night.

I shield my eyes from the opening
as images of me walking with your shadow
in the rain of Seychelles are derived

How blessed can I not be
I observed the sun rising
in the eyes of paradise
So beautiful you are
in the windows of illusions
and of reality.

I may wonder within my silence
even surface upon selfish dreams
Yet no matter the distance you walk unseen
the woman you are
will always be appreciated.

SINCERELY!

'Never Stop'

I never stop dreaming
within the hidden darkness of which I lay
Exploring the fruits of your essence
far beyond the sensual closeness of yesterday
Seemingly, I can't channel
what's sealed in the complexity of my heart
I dream of you with every breath of air I inhale
whether my eyes are open or closed.

Missing you allows me to recognize
and understand what it's like to exist as a phantom to your thoughts
I never stop fantasizing
of sharing another breath of life with you
Experiencing something miraculous and unknown to us both
rendering smiles between the silence of our whispers
that I'm genuinely part of.

I never stop dreaming
of laughing with you
as you rest in my arms reflecting our yesterday
Laying my inner desires on the pillows of your thoughts
while basking in the entanglement we conjure up.

I never stop dreaming
of hearing my name pour from your downy feather lips
Echoing through the deafening silence with royal authority
as I stand before your excellence
beckoning my heart with open arms
Inferno like cravings burn deep within
for the distinctiveness of your irresistible touch
Life is void of light without you.

I never cease to dream of the day
doubt no longer registers upon my thoughts
The moment that I can look into your mesmerizing eyes
and euphoric sensation envelops my body
perfectly as a hyperbaric chamber, and
The day the percussion of our hearts' congas
rhythmically beat as one.

I never stop fantasizing
even through the loneliness crafted by my own ignorance
Even through the emptiness,
silence and flawed illusions.

I never stop fantasizing
of holding you in complete bliss
Fulfilling more than just your inner cravings
aiding in your spiritual elevation
and intellectual growth
'As A Man and Devoted Slave!'

I never stop dreaming
beyond the reality of us holistically
For the definition, central focus and target of my love is 'You.'

I never stop dreaming
of strengthening your belief in me
surrendering all that I am
Walking an endless journey
just to prove that the purity of your air is incomparable

I never stop dreaming
of being blessed to establish life with you.
My love is infinite...

'Seed of Desire'

If you accept nothing of my unseen tears
forever lost
would be the secret whispers of my truth
For I breathe
only the genuine promise of you
Beneath our closest star's radiant beauty.

The window of suspended time
has no criterion reflecting the passion
conquering the governing body of my soul
If I donated my heart
to the Research of Science Institute
The potent existence of my love
could not be detected by the most advanced dissection
For the stealth particles of its origin
are light years more complex.

By the seed
of desired affection spawned through yesterday's touch
I have become as the Birds of Paradise within my own absence
so intriguing to the intellectual thought
That one must study in depth
the distinct beauty of the curvature of your lips
when you smile to envisage me.

"Treasure Undiscovered"

Petals of my love
may fall like leavened tears
For without the nectar of your essence

my roots are only pseudo-nurtured
Denied even the most miniscule progress.

I am a secret that only exists
in the frame of your smile
An Amaryllis
that will wither not
as I grow in my concrete darkness
My Love
my breathing is a by-product of you.

'For You'

For you
I'd extract the wings of my soul
and lay them in a pool of sin
only to watch them emerge as fallen tears in the moon's anti-gravity
Where you'd witness
as our eyes become an exotic state of seduction
That my intentions are pure
and sincere in regards to embracing you holistically.

For you
I'd give myself to the cool stillness of the night
by descending in my nakedness
from the top of Ecuador's volcano's highest peak
Just to photograph 'Nieves Penitent's"
vaporized snow peak
that which the wind cannot imitate.

For you
I'd search amid the secrets
and sleep beneath the surface of the sea
Until I obtained wisdom beyond our world
that astounds your smile
beyond scented candles and cut fruits in the night
hand-held walks through the tunnels of my heart
and petals laid beneath your feet on foreign soil
For my appreciation would never cease.

For you
the mysteries of the star's essence I'd study
far greater than a Dog or warrior
Because, if I couldn't offer you a star itself

then at least I could guide you
without repeating the destinations you've already reached.

For you
I'd willingly surrender
the jewel my mother raised me to be
For a man is only considered a true 'KING'
when he's fortunate to represent
and stand as a reflection of a woman who out measures a "QUEEN."

For you
I'd forbid my blood freedom
and sacrifice the breaths of my soul
from all happiness that's meant to be
to win you over
By making sure your desires realize all that you seek
even if it means I have nothing.

For you
no element of life would come before
In no moment would you exist alone
no breath would I exhale unappreciative of the blessing you are
and never will I cease fighting
'The Governor of Temptation'
of which you are undivided.

For you
I'd never institute what a 'friend' is not
nor hide you from the world or my soul
Because there is no pleasure
in viewing life
when the essence of love is unnoticed
"YOU!"

For you
only the truth of who I am I'd submit

and home I'd be each night
Upon my knees puddled by tears
before the awakening of the twilight
Sincerely showing gratitude to God
for blessing me with His love.

You are the light of true love!

'Today Is The Day'

All praise I surrender to God
For bestowing upon life
A water flower that's far more precious than the air we breathe.

All praise I surrender to God
The creator of existence
Because on this day
He not only granted us mercy by shielding us with his wings
But he defined the essence of His love
By breathing spirit into your lungs
So the beauty of His image could be a testament.

Today is the day
Angels can be seen dancing on the clouds
Below the seventh heavens
The stars' fluorescent sparkle
Outshines the sun at its peak
And time ceases
For only the awakening of your mystique
Overrides impassibility, unlocking the gates of paradise.

My heart is overwhelmed
By every thought of you
Raindrops spiral from heaven
whirling through my hair
As tears salt the earth pressing against my face
Soiling my brows as I offer salat
Surrendering all praise to 'God'
For He so loved the world
He blessed humanity with the mercy of His grace:
You!

Today is the day
I thank God far more than most
Because this is the day
Life sank its talons deep into my heart.

Today is the day
I thank God far more than most
Because this is the day
He merged a diamond with a rose
And gave it life.

Today is the day
God shared the elements with only His breath
To give you life.

'Passion'

My passion for you
enriches my sense of thirst
Beyond the elements of water
and any mere selfish desire
From the constant thoughts of you never altered
($$$$$$$_____$$$$$$$$$$$)
to the physical anomaly exceeding the beauty of all life forms
by your creation.

Greater, you shine within me
than the focused rays of the sun
I have no clear understanding of where I'd be
if the silent whispers of your social grace
did not embed my heart with hunger
But I do know without a doubt
I'd be unable to balance on the high wires of life
or beams of athletic mental stability
Without the effects of your light that burns within me.

My flower
My yearning
I never part with my pillow in the passing moments of the night
For it is all I can embrace
beyond the images
that give me a sense of relief
it's your divineness I'm holding.

I may be emotionally forced
within my physical state of suspension
to live in the cherished memories of our yesterday
For my heart

refuses to accept today
without you genuinely
Sometimes I have the tendency
to open doors of prohibited entry
within my soul
To breathe
as though my inner dreams exist
Yet I know heaven I have not found
for the mesmerizing seduction of your touch
is foreign to my body.

Beautiful
you are known by the eyes of my heart
Irresistible
is your distinguished aura of elegance
Until I breathe the fragrance of your declaration of us
existence will only be physical
But unknown to my love.

Frozen is my soul
without you.

'Priceless Friendship'

The sun shines
even when our eyes only see
the twinkle of a star
Butterflies dance in the wind
even in the moments
we surrender to peace
The sand of the desert
never yields to time
Nor does the fierce waves
of the ocean's roar.

Envision a dove holding a rose in his beak
a glass of water enriched with uncut diamonds
a stallion born with a golden heart
and the beauty of your dimples
stretched in happiness.
Now put them all in a single container of expression
and still all falls short in measuring
the preciousness of friendship and your worth.

I walk alone
beneath the foundation of heaven
Inclining in its pace
instead of mere forward steps
Because
I am driven by a reflection of my inner growth.

God is my superior friend
for He accepts my faults
without judgment.

Mystic smile
we know not each other
beyond words and still captured images
Yet I give you no promise
unyoked of truth
Given the blessed opportunity of knowing you
I will define beyond merit
What God has instilled in me.

Genuine sincerity
and no childish games
Friendship is too precious
to taint with ignorance.
Betrayal and taking you for granted
is not an option.

'Paradise Haven'

Tossed about in the raging waters of my emotions
I struggle day and night through the rapids of loneliness
For the slim chance of basking on the sun soaked shore of your thoughts
and bathing in the privacy of your unimaginable lagoon.

I surrender the treasure of my smile at your feet
for the elegance of your grace
The Caribbean winds of your compassion
confirm that you are the gateway to a haven of tranquility
'A Celestial Heaven, a paradise tucked away in Euphoria.'

I yearn beyond the vessel of my existence
the fallen tears from the wells of my ignorance
and the newly found indescribable understanding of love
Dwelling in the nucleus of my core.

For I lost all
when your belief in me shattered
The eclipsed sun shines darkness upon me
as I stand ungoverned by your woman's worth
but I seek a metropolis unbound, unknown to many
a secret treasure obscured by the laws of nature
An impenetrable haze
protecting the innocent jewel of life itself.

If only I could shine brightly as a supernova
I could burn away the fog, the haze that seals out
all unworthy intruders.

I am but evaporating water yoked by unheated steel.
A cold breeze, a wintry breath yielding no pulse.

By the embedded flame of your beauty, I live
yet I am drained of life far more than physically possible
without ceasing to exist
yet I am only felt when I embrace the lone palm tree of self.

More precious than a Waterford crystal or amethyst
the ethereal nature of my soul cherishes you
If I had a second chance
to stand before you as a selfless man
Principles of Merit... Discipline... and Integrity
those which now define my character
Would truly allow my newly forged impression to shine deep within
the boundaries of your restrictive covering
and burn off the elements veiling your precious lagoon
'For Circumcised Is My Heart'
in the sounds of silence, I lay
Dreaming of sharing mystical triple sized raindrops with you
in your paradise lost.

I thirst for you more
than the river of my desire can quench
Improbable is the chance of reviving my love starved
heart without lifting the cover of fog
To drink but one drop of your healing fountain
for you are the secret chalice filled of my life's elixir
Haze be gone, show me the way to your haven
open your passage way
Expose your lagoon of paradise on earth
unearth the key to my existence
for you are my life flower.

'Infinite Passion'

Against the currents of Jizhaigou mystic waters
the burning of my obsession
has me walking upstream
Puncturing God's air
with unwavering missiles of kisses
As I declare war in pursuit of your happiness.

Perched
high upon hand woven Zimbabwe wool
I find you
in between the shades of day and night
Secretly drawing closed
the hidden gates of your smile.

Unknown
are the steps of my arrival
The sensuous display
of 'Infinite Passion'
I enhance as I carve a French kiss
into the fruit of your neck
with the enticing strokes of my tongue
Mildly startling you
and I apologize not for desiring you sincerely.

Unheard are the felt echoes of my heart
tattooing its password upon your back
Your eyes, I blind seductively
with the veil
of my inner invisible truth
While slightly arching and turning your head

whereupon I infuse your lips
With the reduction sauce of my soul.

You make me feel without thought
that you are the air I breathe
My happiness, I'd surrender
never to exist
void of your embrace.

The enchanting whispers of falling water
causes us to become victims
of fire that emits no light
Mystic smile
please don't hurt me
For I am a virgin
who is sensitive of failure.

Never
have I been exposed to love
Teach me
because dreams fall short of the affection
I desire to achieve with you
Teach me
to embolden my reality.

'Award Me'

Award me the opportunity to fail
the ability to wither
as a fallen leaf in time
Award me the pleasure
of losing your treasure
For given the cries of my inner hunger
no footsteps of yesterday will I follow, and
Expectations
I will travel above.

Consider me a selfish liar
one who's conniving, controlling, abusive
and stands upon manipulation that renders no respect
Consider me a misguided fool
one who lacks self-understanding
and whose character is defined as less than a man
View me as a reflection of undesired pain
and I will cut open the veins of my wrist
Whereupon the sincerity of my invisible truth
which lies dormant in my blood
Would flow in between the breaths of your insecurities
and my tears
Proving with every drop that shortens my life
your trust and belief
I am worth.

Believe not in me
if you're comfortable with disappointment
and would hate me for taking it away
Open not the sexy gates of your eyes
if emptiness and deception

are the visions you seek
For my handsomeness
offers so much more
Turn away from me
allowing silence to be the achievement gained
If the fruits of sin
be the thirst of your yearning.

Free my soul
and in time, I will find my way home
Hold my hand
and your heart will call me
"INFINITE"
Award me the opportunity to fail
and our breaths
would never be unyoked of the same air
Just think of me
and I'll yield no pleasure from time
Failure
I will never accomplish with you.

'Would You Still Believe In My Love'

My tears appear diluted
as they descend from my eyes
and what I cherish as love
Seemingly feels like a contaminated dream.

I submitted my soul to your soul
yet internally I feel as though I've failed.
Why does it seem I'm forgotten?

Glancing out my window
scintillating, shimmering lights
Filled with celestial beauty of which no tongue can describe
allow me to peer into the marrow of my soul through
the hollows of my darkness
It seemed as if my soul was crawling erratically beside my feet
as though it were searching for the fallen shrapnel of my heart.

The sun shines upon me
yet rigorously I shake as though I'm naked in frigid weather
I hold myself only to feel nothing of significance.

If I sheltered myself in the warmth of another woman's embrace
and closed my eyes to two-time comfort.
"Would You Still Believe In My Love?"
"A Burning Passion, Pure and Immeasurable."

No matter the season I walk alone
for my destination is your fulfillment
'Surrendered Is My Soul'

By the sincerity that promised to infinitely stand as one
will the gates of your heart
Still retract for my presence unconditionally
if I began sharing who I am with someone else
Allowing uncommon affection to be seeded
as seductive expression frolicked
and acceptance began to be governed.
'Would You Still Believe In My Love?'
'A Burning Passion, Pure and Immeasurable.'

My inner loneliness has no definition...

My excuse for being weak in my submission
is self-fear that you will stop loving me(#$$$$$$$$$$$$$$$$)
And Believing in us.

I dream to escape a confined emptiness
that checks me with the emotional realization
'I am forgotten'
Precious defines all that you render
for special is what you telegraph.

Would you turn from me as the wind
if you came to learn
That I substituted your genuine embrace
to give assurance to my selfishness
And not only allowed her who is not you
to gracefully caress the fibers of my face with her fingers
As the internal stimulation brings our cravings closer
whereas we become lost in kisses that do not fade.
'Would You Still Believe In My Love?'
'A Burning Passion, Pure and Immeasurable.'

Your smile is the replica of my heart
the only life symbol scripted upon my soul.

Would you still believe in my love
if I laid flowers at the feet of another woman
Until I was fortunate enough to solidify my dream
of defining life with you and only you?

'I Yearn'

My dream of holding the life blessing you are
under the sun
Emotionally kissing your thoughts
and laying the origin of my soul
Laced with lily petals beneath your feet
and no empty thoughts I cling to for comfort
While tossing and turning in the loneliness of the night
winded, panting for air soaked by my optic waterfall.

Life's Blessing, I am thrust back in the midst of cherished memories
of your authenticated approval
Symbolic of thoughts of me is ($$$$$$$$$$$$$$$$$)
the strength of your smile in all its glory and warmth
Yet, seriously, you must understand
it's thinking about who you are
and that defined by the calmness of your posture and gestures
($$$$$$$$$$$$$)
That give exceptional meaning to the cloaked secrecy of passion
burning in the folds of my desire.

I yearn to feed you fruit
offering your life embellished substance
Immensely more intensified than the affection
which swipes a brushstroke of your past on canvas
and stokes the furnace of my dreams.

I yearn to read untold knowledge to your heart
openly conveying who I am beyond the acoustical impression
of tears whispering in the current of the wind
Like the sound of wings flapping.

Life's Blessing, I yearn to establish a measure of sincerity with you
that which the deepest depth of the ocean could not compress
My hands have never caressed a jewel more precious
than the colorful diamond you are
Nor were my emotions born to Utopia
before your touch spawned extreme life within me
As scorched earth I existed
until the warmth of your sensuality rained down on me.

My Flower
you are who and that which
incites a riot in my desires raging uncontrollably
showing unstoppable longing for
"You, My Favored Blessing of God!"

I miss so much of the enriching signature your warmth once afforded me
for now, I only have what I conjure up of a distant you in silence
Self concocted dreams poured up unaccompanied, 80 proof
that give our now nullified embrace reason
and genuine closeness that's woven by
Trust.. Respect.. Honesty.. Loyalty.. Dignity.. and open Communication.

Life's Blessing, my flesh runs to you
yet my soul crawls with grace
For no matter the distance or silence
my desires will always be guided
By the beacon of your integrity.

I may journey upon my own beliefs
that lays my head in your hands
But it's not of a dream cherished or lost
that governs your smile with my love
For in truth
I've carved your name into my spine
With the arteries of my soul
"INFINITE"

One day your persona will graduate
no longer swimming only in a school of fishy illusions.

'Submission'

The element of time
Always unearths the hidden
Of its secret existence
For no darkness shines infinitely.

That's why
I never stop believing
in the love chastening my tongue
I cry, for it seems
my destination has no arrival
Yet I will forever crawl upon bended knees
because I've learned
That no realized desire is greater
nor will it culminate a more fulfilled meaning
sustained over time with reason
When the consequence is losing you.

There is no lie in the truth
that's why I lay my heart at your feet.

My Love
I miss the feeling of pleasure
surging through my veins
Whenever the tenderness of your fingers
found a lonely part of my spirit to caress.

My sense of thought becoming lost
as I held the flower of you in my arms
While bonding in selfish seduction
with the exotic sweetness of your lips.

In truth
I still lay by myself
and drift to whispers of your softness
Cherished in the gates of my canals.

Beautiful Butterfly
you are the door of my love
invisible yet sincere
Yes, your beacon
dictates my direction
If I sheltered the truth of my inner passion
in the same significance of a water lily
Or more natural
to that of your eyes' mesmerizing beauty
My love would forever be lost
in Travesty Lake fed by a spring of tears
Just as I am emotionally without you.

LOST!!!

This morning I awoke
by messengers of rain
descending upon my heart
As joyful pain
pitter-patted the fabric of my face
Only because I dreamed you said
'I Love You'

I am light years away emotionally
from understanding the true depths of my love
But I do understand without question
why I feel Doves circulating in my soul
Whenever thoughts of you invade my loneliness.

Continuously I will journey through the storm
poised without fear
Submitted to my dreams of you.

Chains of selfishness
may separate our affection
and I'm sorry for my ignorance
But wholeheartedly I convey
that I will, never unveil my soul
In the interest of another
for my submission governs you.

'If You'

If you could journey within the hidden tunnels of my mind
Discovering untold secrets and reasons
Why the sensuous essence of your being
Fades not from the core of my thoughts.
Would you think of me
At least in your moments of boredom?

If you could look through the shallow gateways of my eyes
Scrutinizing my starched principles, untainted ethics
And sincere desire for you
Without extinguishing your fiery divinity
For a fragment of your spirit is entwined with the loneliness entrenched
Between the walls of my soul.
Would you think of me
At least in your moments of boredom?

If I could reach from the shadows of my own darkness
Under empty stands that suppress our existence
And enable you to surface the true significance of your being
Within the pipeline of my fiber
By caressing the softness of your identity with my fingers.
Would you think of me
At least in your moments of boredom?

If I whispered enchantingly in your ear
The reasons why your existence envelopes my life
Every detail truly absorbed
With such intuit and prestige.
Would you think of me
At least in your moments of boredom?

If I could embrace the tender texture of your miraculous essence
Unsuspending hidden desires in fierce rafters
Yet wither not in physical structure
Upon the chemical reaction created by the euphoric connection of our
flesh
'One Perfect Bond of Union' physically sustained.
Would you think of me
Even in your moments of boredom?

If I rained down no further tears
Externally or internally upon facing my reflection
Without the assurance of your mesmerizing smile
Nor continuously dreamed
Within the endless silence of my own dreams
And extracted the punctured lining of my heart yielding no blood
While placing its delicate essence in the palm of your hand
Whereas you witness beyond my faintness of breath
At the center of its mass
A breathtaking rose embedded
Upon which your name is inscribed.
Would you think of me
At least in your moments of boredom?

'No Excuse'

No excuse is given for the ignorance of my past
the meaning lost by your closeness detached
the emptiness I've gained standing unknown and alone
For every man that has abused your compassion
lied continuously to be warmed by the hypnotic beauty of your smile
and has guided you nowhere beyond cheap intimacy and broken dreams
Openly, I apologize for the stupidity
and selfish ignorance of us all.

If I could wipe away the source of your fallen tears
yesterday's regrets would no longer have an origin
and your tribulations would wither
For reasons desired beyond my own disrespect
I'd subscribe by the will of a genuine presence
the completeness of my existence to your every need.

From the emptiness of which I lay hidden
I reach not to find meaningless refuge
in the comfort of your thoughts
Only to embed the truth
that the hole in my heart cries aloud
For I miss beyond the definition of words
the precious warmth of 'Your Embrace.'

Life has many phases
truly your attraction to me accounts for one
If I could wipe away your fallen thoughts
selfish, manipulative, nor conniving would be your vision of me
Broken elements would never descend
pleasure would no longer be lost by ignorance
and I would never put my desires before your own
If I could wipe away your fallen thoughts

you would come to learn
That my cry is sincere
I only fear you not knowing I love you.

Silence may comfort me in my loneliness
yet my passion is filled to capacity
and it strengthens me
I look beyond myself when I substitute my rogue thoughts
with sensuous thoughts of you
My soul is your secret shadow
for you are my fountain of life
my unanticipated inspiration
Even though my emotions remain foreign to your senses
still I dream upon every ounce of you
My love will never evaporate.

"NEVER"

'Your Body Is Mine'

If you awoke in the dwindling twilight
By the stealthy silence of me standing admiring your preciousness
Wrapped in the linen of my nakedness
Erecting only to whisper 'I love you'
As your eyes widened to the surprise of me
Would you scream aloud
Or open your arms to my vulnerability.

If I saddened you by an issue small in merit
Could I be punished not with your silence or anger
Of which may deter our cravings
But yet chastise my tongue to submission as a slave
To desires governed by your command
Stimulating an intense infusion of our flesh
That spikes you with pleasure far greater than conceivable?

Is it possible beyond reason that I could seduce your erotic psyche
By arousing the sensitivity of your nipples
Until they stand rigidly at attention
Intrigue the outer walls of your hidden treasure
Or the softness of your lips with the wetness of my tongue
As you bite sensually into your bottom lip?
'I Just Want To Entice You Enough To Call Out My Name!'

If I clasped your hips firmly from the back
Then pulled your upper body within my chest
In an embrace that allowed you to feel
Our hearts beating rhythmically in sync
While massaging the center of your neck and back
With intimate passion that causes you to whisper my name
Would the warmth of your nectar flow upon my love

So hungry I am
Can I taste you?

I wonder what it feels like to climb
Inside the narrow gates of your garden
As you hang partially from the bed
Reaching out to me with increasing affection.

I wonder what it feels like
To penetrate your slippery quarters, climb inside you
Arching your back
And gliding deeper and deeper into your sensuous abyss.

I wonder what it feels like to climb inside of you
As you touch and spread your own wings
Staring at me with glazed eyes
And you pull me close to introduce my tongue to your lips.

As I caress while teasing and tasting
The exotic sweetness of your thick wet lips
Then a pausing whisper, "I love you" from Australia
The Land Down Under.

One day
I will kiss your navel
Foreshadowing erotic incremental pleasures to come
Then slip between your moist inner thighs
To define my tongue as more potent than heroin
Carving my name on your hidden
Hollywood Walls of Flame
Forever etched in your memory.

One day
I will kiss the heart of your artichoke
Then skinny dip in the middle of your ocean
Diving Into Caribbean waves of aquatic thermal sensation

Merging my soul with the love you cry.
Spellbound, I watch, hypnotized by the pendulum of your hips
swinging back and forth
across the focal point of my privileged eyes.

One day
I will no longer be trapped in a dream of loving you
Until then
I submit my heart as I stand alone
Rising and setting each day
Touched by rays of our distant sun.

'Memories'

All I have to comfort loneliness
are memories of our yesterday
cherished thoughts of every nuance of you never fading
As I lounge in moments of your perfection
adoration knows
that my heart wants you back
beyond a level that spoken words can express
Your tantalizing touch, the warmth of your comfort
the sincerity of your support, and commitment.

So little by little, I pray each day
as I yearn in silence for your return
'I Miss You More Than I Miss Myself'
sometimes I find myself laughing
caught up in shared moments once endured between us
while shedding tears that fill my lungs with no outlet.

Thoughts of our yesterday always suppress
the loneliness growing in the deep surface of my heart
Even though I failed you
just as those before me who shared your extravagant aura
My ignorance often formed self-pity within
for I misunderstood life and self
without realizing I'd be losing you to an accomplishment
undesirable.... nothingness.

I acted like a wild child
paralyzed of sound direction
that's why it's so easy for me to understand
why you refuse to lower your standards once more
Truly I appreciate you beyond my actions

beyond mere words
and even beyond what's detectable in the depths of my heart.

One of a kind, you are
and irreplaceable, you will infinitely be
I may have showed that I was unprepared
for the genuine sweetness of your warmth
Yet my memories
nor my desires of love at bay shall ever die.

I am thankful to have been in your thoughts once more...
I am grateful to have been fortunate to hold you within my arms...
I realize that I was blessed kissing your lips and holding your hand...
I may have failed
but I have not surrendered
I will never throw in the towel
I remain on course for the destination of you.

You are the Irresistible rose of my heart
and I broadcast your true woman's worth as appreciated
I will only stop believing in you
when I'm able to turn back the hands of time
Until then I imagine, I crawl, I walk, I run
towards what separates us with the noise of silence.

'Separated'

Every moment that we're separated by polarizing forces
and the torturous silence I desire not
crescendos without boundary to a thunderous roar
I brush your name across my iris
with the tip of the wing of a fluttering Palos Verses Blue
Oooh if only the sincerity of my heart were audible as it whispers
you would hear and feel the pulsating seduction
powering my journey in a magnificent dream
Or maybe somehow feel the vibrations of my passion that burns
like a California wildfire under the soles of your footsteps
Then my decoy would no longer mask my secret
exposed would be the truth, center stage
curtains polarized as I stand stark naked of all deception
vulnerable as I am drawn to your celestial glow.

Days have passed
shared thoughts often seem lost
vivid memories are all I have left
Yet still I wonder
while mentally painting your smile
on the canvas of a Ceylon Rose
Has desire for us trapped itself within your temporal confines
exiling me to the center of forgotten isle.($$$$$$$$$$$$$$)

I yearn to watch your breasts reflect in the twilight again.
I yearn to get lost in your eyes and never be found.

Last night I slow-danced in the rain
with your curvaceous silhouette
Spellbound, I watched, hypnotized by the pendulum of your hips
swinging back and forth

across the focal point of my privileged eyes
If only you could see
how beautiful you are in that vision, that glorious scene
'A Colorless Diamond of Pure Clarity'
would merely seem as shattered glass in comparison.

If I have failed
to be prevalent in the preciousness of your love
or at least spring a simple thought
At least know that you have prevailed
because the refreshing breath of my tongue
parades as a banner of irrefutable belief in you
Surrendering to the voice of an angel
and streaming tears for the taste of your savory hors d'oeuvres
Respectfully
my desire to stand downwind of the innocence of your fragrance
will never trace the meaning of a fleeting thought
For your aroma is the pure essence and flavor of authentic love.

No matter the decibels of deafening silence screaming between us
I will not be mute
Committed I am, to a Love Chant bringing life to my dream.

'I Breathe'

Passion brews and swells within my kettle
Stimulating thirst for the taste of your frothiness
I long for the rejuvenation of my chapped lips
Saturate me with your lusciousness
I miss you Red Diamond
And the trickling blood creating a passage in my heart confirms it.

So depressing it is to face each day
Denied the enticement of your veil of whispers
If only you knew what I knew
Or could see what I see
Familiar to your assurance would ultimately define love
Tucked away in my heart.

I want to discover endless affection with you
And I only expect you to understand
I breathe to prove
"I Love You Beautiful"
Now... Then... and Tomorrow...

How can I not desire you
When you complete my destination
I cherish the intention of your smile
Even as I yearn for the sincerity of your unreplaceable embrace
Warm... Potent... and Unchangeable...
You are a Galaxy rose without origin
Beauty without end.

Gorgeous, my emotions are not selfish cries of loneliness
Nor a dream empty of substance

Sincerely, you are my heart
And the reason love is sown on the fallow ground of my soul.

Doubt may comfort you
Disbelief may inflate
Yet I will never stop fighting
For the life pleasure of being your emotional puppet
A slave that honors your acceptance
And committed to respecting your woman's worth.

It is to you I surrender my loyalty
Compassion.. Sincerity.. Attention.. Honesty.. and Appreciation
It is to you my soul runs
Because in truth
It is you my cries target with shrapnel
Hoping to pierce the veil of desire for you
I truly live to embrace you eternally
Breathe the air that you breathe
For I shall not falter in securing your trust
I will not fail to govern myself with the purity of your heart
I want you...

'Silently I Whisper'

When I open my eyes
to the moonlight aglow
And the bosomed passion
glistens among inner drifts of mist
silently I whisper to myself
'So Mystical and Beautiful You Are.'

When I stand
unenveloped by the dreams of your smile
Mirror polished by clouds and wind
and the spring's rain
becomes the sensuous essence of your touch
Secretly I scribble across my heart
'So Beautiful You Are.'

My thoughts fall like snowflakes
in a summer sun rise
upon the hidden seeds of my yearning
Whenever I envision
guarding your shadow in the night
laying long stemmed purple roses on your pillow
for your eyes' awakening
Or fanning your warmth
with feathers from the wings of an angel
I stole in a dream
Silently I whisper as your footsteps invade my thoughts
'So Beautiful You Are.'

When the secrets have faded
the tears of loneliness have ceased
the chains yoking my lungs have rusted

and my worries of you
no longer stain my heart
'Dusted in Winter White'
Silently I whisper to myself
'So Beautiful You Are.'

Absent of thought
you are the exotic butterfly
that dances above
'The Five Flower Lake'
My most cherished dream within this life and the next
as I blow kisses to your picture sitting in my window
secretly, I whisper to myself
'I Love You.'

'I Hunger'

Dreaming of you is not an empty fantasy I ponder upon
to give me a sense of life in my castle of darkness
Truly my love
you are missed in more significant areas
than just my thoughts, the canals of my heart, and the depths of my soul.

Baby
you are my strength
my vision, my smile and reason to exist
I hunger voraciously for the day
I'm fortunate enough to look in the gateways of your eyes
and witness the self belief of my contained emotions
I hunger
for the pleasures granted by God
of sharing a plutonic night with you
as we mentally entwine
staring far into the horizon while enhancing our acquaintance
I hunger ravenously
within the wilderness of my heart
to share with the genuineness of your acceptance
The definition of my soul
and to define the internal passion you've cultivated in my veins
even though the cherished image of your smile comforts me silently
Still I suffer miserably
living my life absent of you.

When it's dark
and the pain throbbing from lingering upon you so greatly increases
I often count the liquid measures of your steps

as you walk towards me in my dreams.

The illusions of you embracing my heart gives me inner peace.

I hunger immensely
for the opportunity to line my arms with your softness
and say without fear
Or an expansion of the feelings you've spawned
by sharing a life with me in my dreams
"Life's Blessing, I Love You."

Your fragrant love fills my lungs in the 'LIGHT'
for you are the catalyst of my emotions
The definition within my steps
the purpose I cry for internally
I hunger greatly
for the moment that we both open our eyes fulfilled
and thank God for guiding us to the destination of sufficient togetherness
'LOVE.'

My Queen
I will only stop missing you
in the seconds my heart skips a beat
for in the brevity of that moment
The warmth of your smile envelopes me
and I find myself holistically a part of you
'I Love You Beyond What I Understand'
"INFINITELY!"

'Appreciated'

Your woman's worth
Is appreciated beyond the realm of infatuation
Or a delusional thought
Even more, an infinite fantasy sustained
In the howling corridors of the wind
Your woman's worth
Magnifies life
And hovers above the sun.

I dream a dream
In a dream
Of a dream
That grants me not even a faint image
Beyond the visage of your delicate smile.

"BREATHLESS"
Is so beneath the class of beauty which characterizes you.

Sincerity exceeds the inferno of my sweltering passion
Mentally, I bleed
For the knowledge of who you are
For the amassing of your strength
Your understanding..... Your peace.....
The [EV] O-LU*TION of your womanhood
Now, then, and to come
Mentally, I bleed
For the blessing of looking into your eyes
Without dreaming.

I think you're precious
Not just a distinction of uniqueness

A infinite mirror of magnificence
Truly, I believe
Special is your atmosphere.

Why
Is honestly tomorrow's question
What's far more important now
Is that you submit to defining the birth of you
And accept without justification
Appreciated, you are
Sincerely by far.

The End

Iqra Publishing Inc

www.ingramcontent.com/pod-product-compliance
Lightning Source LLC
Chambersburg PA
CBHW060427050426
42449CB00009B/2174